Table of Contents

Intelligence/Investigations Function Guidance

The National Incident Management System (NIMS) represents a core set of doctrine, concepts, principles, terminology, and organizational processes that enables effective, efficient, and collaborative incident management. The Incident Command System (ICS), as a component of NIMS, establishes a consistent operational framework that enables government, private sector, and nongovernmental organizations to work together to manage incidents, regardless of cause, size, location, or complexity. This consistency provides the foundation for the use of ICS for all incidents, ranging from daily occurrences to incidents requiring a coordinated Federal response.

Many domestic incidents, such as natural disasters or industrial accidents, have an obvious cause and origin. However, other domestic incidents, such as large-scale fires, public health emergencies, explosions, transportation incidents (e.g., train derailments, airplane crashes, bridge collapses), active shooters, terrorist attacks, or other incidents causing mass injuries or fatalities, require an intelligence or investigative component to determine the cause and origin of the incident and/or support incident/disaster operations.

The scalability and flexibility of NIMS allows the Intelligence/Investigations (I/I) Function to be seamlessly integrated with the other functions of ICS. The I/I Function within ICS provides a framework that allows for the integration of intelligence and information collection, analysis, and sharing, as well as investigations that identify the cause and origin of an incident regardless of source. If the incident is determined to be a criminal event, the I/I Function leads to the identification, apprehension, and prosecution of the perpetrator. The I/I Function can be used for planned events as well as incidents.

This document includes guidance on how various disciplines can use and integrate the I/I Function while adhering to NIMS concepts and principles. It includes information intended for the NIMS practitioner (including the Incident Commander/Unified Command [IC/UC]) that assists in the placement of the I/I Function within the command structure; provides guidance that may be used while implementing the I/I Function; and has an accompanying Intelligence/Investigations Function Field Operations Guide (I/I FFOG). While this document provides an example of the I/I Function at the Section level, the IC/UC has the final determination of the scope and placement of the I/I Function within the command structure. The guidance provided in this document is applicable for both domestic incidents that use conventional unclassified information (e.g., open source information, criminal histories, medical records, or educational records)[1] and terrorism incidents where information is often classified and requires the use of national intelligence capabilities.

For the purpose of this document, information and intelligence should be interpreted broadly to support user needs across all-threats and all-hazards environments to prevent, protect against, mitigate, respond to, and recover from the effects of incidents, regardless of cause, size, location,

---

[1] Such information must be accessed only in compliance with relevant local, state, and Federal laws.

or complexity.[2] The activities and information that are at the core of the I/I Function have historically been viewed as the primary responsibilities of "traditional" law enforcement departments and agencies at all levels of government. Although, in many cases, law enforcement departments/agencies fulfill intelligence/investigations duties, the I/I Function has aspects that cross disciplines and levels of government. "Nontraditional" forms of intelligence/investigations activities (i.e., non-law enforcement) might include:

- Epidemiology

- Mass fatality management

- Fire, explosion, or arson cause and origin (regardless of likelihood of criminal activity)

- Real-time research and analysis intended to protect against, respond, and/or recover from a specific incident (e.g., critical infrastructure vulnerability and consequence analysis; hurricane forecast regarding strength and estimated point of landfall; post-earthquake technical clearinghouse; or post-alert volcanic monitoring)

- Transportation accidents.

This document can be used by jurisdictions and agencies when developing new plans for establishing the I/I Function or when incorporating the I/I Function into existing plans. Users of this document are encouraged to tailor its content, including the information and model in the I/I FFOG, to reflect jurisdiction authorities and/or incident needs.

This document contains a recommended organizational framework for executing the I/I Function. The I/I Guide provides neither legal authority nor direction and does not supersede applicable legal authorities and constraints at any jurisdictional level. Personnel managing and performing intelligence and investigations activities must always comply with applicable authorities, statutes, law, ordinances, regulations, and policies within and affecting their jurisdiction and/or agency. This document informs Command and General Staff personnel who are responsible for making strategic and operational decisions during an incident. The guidance provided in this document does not empower or authorize personnel to take on roles or responsibilities for which they are not authorized, trained, or certified, nor does it substitute for training in the proper tactics, techniques, and procedures related to performing intelligence- and investigations-related operations functions and activities. Users should consult their agency counsel to determine applicable authorities.

Additionally, intelligence and investigations practitioners must protect constitutional, victim, and privacy rights, civil rights, and civil liberties; restrict the dissemination of sensitive/classified information; and honor legally imposed restrictions on investigative behavior that affect the admissibility of evidence and the credibility of witnesses.

---

[2] Intelligence gathered within the I/I Function is information that either leads to the detection, prevention, apprehension, and prosecution of criminal activities, or the individuals involved, including terrorist incidents or information that leads to determination of the cause of a given incident (regardless of the source), such as public health events or fires with unknown origins. (Federal Emergency Management Agency, National Incident Management System, December 2008)

Introduction

NIMS provides a systematic, proactive approach guiding local, state, tribal, territorial, insular area, and Federal governments; the private sector; and nongovernmental organizations to work seamlessly to prevent, protect against, mitigate, respond to, and recover from the effects all threats and hazards. NIMS is based on the premise that the use of a common incident management framework provides emergency management and response personnel a standardized system for emergency management and incident response activities.

Presidential Policy Directive (PPD) 8 describes the Nation's approach to national preparedness. The National Preparedness Goal is the cornerstone for the implementation of PPD-8; identified within it are the Nation's core capabilities across five mission areas: Prevention, Protection, Mitigation, Response, and Recovery. The National Preparedness System is the instrument employed to build, sustain, and deliver those core capabilities in order to achieve the goal of a secure and resilient Nation. The National Planning Frameworks, which are part of the National Preparedness System, set the strategy and doctrine for building, sustaining, and delivering the core capabilities. The maturation and use of NIMS helps ensure that a unified approach across all mission areas as the National Preparedness System is implemented.

Pursuant to NIMS, a single set of objectives is developed for the entire incident, and a collective approach is used to develop strategies to achieve incident objectives. All agencies with responsibility for the incident have an understanding of joint priorities and restrictions, and no agency's legal authorities are compromised or neglected. The combined efforts of all agencies are optimized as they perform their respective assignments under a single Incident Action Plan (IAP).

Most incidents are managed locally and typically do not need assistance from other jurisdictions; however, some incidents may begin with a single response within a single jurisdiction and rapidly expand to multidisciplinary, multijurisdictional levels requiring significant additional resources, including Federal resources. Neither NIMS nor this I/I Function guidance changes the investigation of the cause of certain domestic incidents within the jurisdiction of specific Federal agencies. For example, the National Transportation Safety Board investigates airline, rail, and other transportation accidents. The Federal Bureau of Investigation (FBI), within the United States, leads criminal investigations involving terrorist acts and terrorist threats by individuals or groups, as well as related intelligence collection activities.[3]

The following sections address how the I/I Function can be incorporated into each NIMS component.

Preparedness

Prior to the start of a planned event (e.g., parade, concert, convention, sporting event, or National Special Security Event), the I/I Function can be used to foster information sharing and

---

[3] The FBI Joint Operations Center, National Transportation Safety Board Command Post, U.S. Secret Service Multi-Agency Coordination Center, and Bureau of Alcohol, Tobacco, Firearms, and Explosives Critical Incident Management Response Team, for instance, would be the "NIMS-compliant" structures managing the I/I Function. Pursuant to Federal law, Federal regulations, and Presidential Directives and Executive Orders, the Attorney General of the United States, generally acting through the FBI, will coordinate the activities of the other members of the law enforcement community to detect, prevent, preempt, and disrupt terrorist attacks against the United States. For additional information, see the National Prevention Framework.

collaboration. It can also provide the information and intelligence necessary to ensure that planning activities are fully informed. Furthermore, as the result of a credible threat of criminal or terrorist activity, an intelligence/investigations organization may be activated and operations may be initiated prior to the occurrence of an incident. If an incident subsequently occurs, the I/I Function should incorporate the appropriate elements of the pre-incident intelligence/ investigations organization, and use the pre-incident information and intelligence that was collected. It is vital to plan for the possibility that an incident may escalate beyond the resources of a local community. Therefore, preparedness activities should include planning for the response of Federal resources and personnel. Activities should also include the transfer of primary investigative and prosecutive jurisdiction and responsibility from local to Federal agencies consistent with applicable laws, regulations, and policies.

Communications and Information Management

Effective emergency management and incident response activities rely on flexible communications and information systems to provide a common operating picture to emergency management/response personnel. Planning for communications and information management should address the policies and procedures, equipment, systems, standards, and training necessary to achieve integrated communications.

Of particular importance to the I/I Function is having information management systems in place, as well as having the means necessary to safeguard information (e.g., information security protocols). Important aspects of information management include identification of and familiarization with communications systems, tools, procedures, and methods. Those operating the I/I Function should ensure that necessary types of information and/or intelligence—including but not limited to voice, data, image, and text—are shared among appropriate personnel (i.e., people with appropriate clearance, access, and need to know) in an authorized manner (i.e., appropriate information technology system). They should also work together to protect personally identifiable information, understanding the different combination of laws, regulations, and other mandates under which various local, state, tribal, territorial, insular area, and Federal agencies operate.[4]

Resource Management

Resource management involves the coordination, oversight, and processes that provide for the timely employment of resources during an incident. Ensuring that resource management systems and procedures are in place prior to an incident (or a planned event) is crucial to acquiring the resources necessary during an incident. Resource management is integral to intelligence/ investigations activities as a means of providing logistical support, credentialing personnel prior to incidents, and badging of emergency management and incident response personnel during incidents.

---

[4] Personally identifiable information is any information about an individual maintained by an agency, including (1) any information that can be used to distinguish or trace an individual's identity, such as name, social security number, date and place of birth, mother's maiden name, or biometric records; and (2) any other information that is linked or linkable to an individual, such as medical, educational, financial, and employment information. (National Institute of Standards and Technology, U.S. Department of Commerce, Special Publication 800-122, Guide to Protecting the Confidentiality of Personally Identifiable Information [2010])

Command and Management

The ICS, Multiagency Coordination Systems, and Public Information are the fundamental elements of incident management. These elements provide standardization through consistent terminology and established organizational structures. The collection, analysis, and dissemination of incident-related information and intelligence are aspects of ICS. The I/I Function provides several critical benefits to an IC/UC, such as:

- Ensuring that:
  - Information and intelligence of tactical value is collected, exploited, and disseminated to resolve an imminent threat or prevent an imminent attack or follow-on attacks
  - Intelligence/investigations activities are managed and performed in a coordinated manner to prevent the inadvertent and inappropriate:
    - Creation of multiple, conflicting investigative records
    - Use of different evidence processing protocols
    - Interviews of the same person multiple times by different personnel
    - Use of different evidence invoicing and chain of custody procedures
    - Detention or arrest of suspects
    - Surveillance of suspects
    - Analysis of forensic or digital and multimedia evidence using different methodologies
  - An IC/UC has the personnel with the subject matter expertise to conduct necessary intelligence/investigations operations
- Providing:
  - An IC/UC with open source, sensitive, and classified information and intelligence in a manner similar to how these types of information would be made available to other authorized and properly cleared personnel who may be responding to the incident
  - A means of linking directly to Federal command centers, such as the National Transportation Safety Board's Command Post or the FBI's Joint Operations Center, to provide for continual information sharing and the seamless transfer of the I/I Function as needed
  - Coordination with other information sharing entities, including state or major urban area fusion centers, Regional Intelligence Sharing Systems (RISS) Centers, High Intensity Drug Trafficking Area Investigative Support Centers, Joint Terrorism Task Forces, and other analytic and investigative entities as applicable
  - Access to information sharing tools and portals, such as the Emergency Management and Response–Information Sharing and Analysis Center (EMR–ISAC),[5] the Homeland

---

[5] The EMR-ISAC is a component of Federal Emergency Management Agency/U.S. Fire Administration that provides critical information analysis, sanitizes classified or sensitive information, and distributes it nationally to thousands of emergency response and management entities.

Security Information Network (HSIN),[6] RISS,[7] Law Enforcement Online (LEO),[8] and other information sharing systems

- Allowing an IC/UC to determine whether the incident is the result of criminal acts or terrorism; make and adjust operational decisions accordingly; and maximize efforts to prevent additional criminal activities or terrorism

- As permitted by local, state, tribal, territorial, insular area, and Federal law, allowing an IC/UC to initiate intelligence/investigations activities while ensuring that life safety operations remain the primary incident objective (see Figure 1). The I/I Function operates concurrently with, and in support of, life safety operations to protect evidence at crime and investigative scenes.

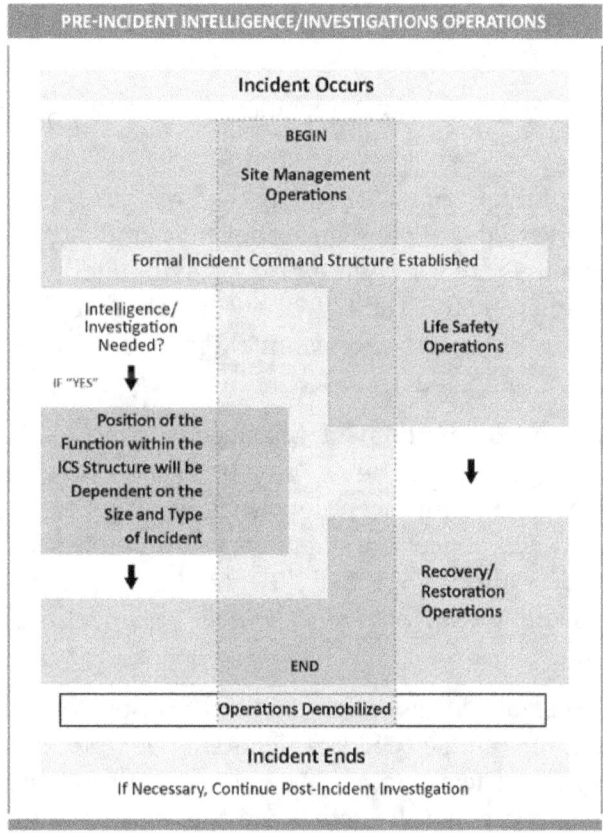

Figure 1: Example of the Flow of Events in Establishing the Intelligence/Investigations Function

---

[6] HSIN is a comprehensive, nationally secure and trusted Web-based platform used to facilitate Sensitive But Unclassified information sharing and collaboration between local, state, tribal, Federal, private sector, and international partners.

[7] The RISS Program is composed of six regional projects that share intelligence and coordinate efforts against criminal networks operating in many locations across jurisdictional lines. Although the six RISS projects are primarily focused on drug crime, they may select additional target crimes and provide a range of services to assist their member agencies.

[8] LEO is an online controlled-access communications and information sharing data repository. It provides an Internet-accessible focal point for electronic Sensitive But Unclassified communication and information sharing for international, local, state, tribal, and Federal law enforcement agencies.

Intelligence/Investigations Function

The mission of the I/I Function is to ensure that all intelligence/investigations operations and activities are properly managed, coordinated, and directed in order to:

- Prevent/Deter potential unlawful activity, incidents, and/or attacks

- Collect, process, analyze, secure, and appropriately disseminate information and intelligence

- Identify, document, process, collect, create a chain of custody for, safeguard, examine, analyze, and store probative evidence

- Conduct a thorough and comprehensive investigation that leads to the identification, apprehension, and prosecution of the perpetrators

- Serve as a conduit to provide situational awareness (local and national) pertaining to an incident

- Inform and support life safety operations, including the safety and security of all response personnel.

To accomplish the mission of the I/I Function, the IC/UC will determine the incident objectives and strategies and then prioritize them. These priorities may shift as an incident changes. Ultimately, life safety operations are the highest priority, with intelligence/investigations operations being initiated concurrently. The IC/UC ensures that provisions are made for the safety, health, and security of responders and that intelligence/investigations operations contribute toward a safer, healthier, and more secure life safety operation.

In today's multi-hazard and threat environment, response personnel should consider all potential causes of an incident (e.g., accidental, criminal, or natural) and take the necessary steps to preserve potential evidence and/or crime scenes while protecting life safety. To efficiently and effectively develop and use intelligence/investigations information, the I/I Function is integrated into the ICS structure. The ICS allows for scalability and the IC/UC has the flexibility to establish the I/I Function within the incident management organizational structure based upon the nature and type of incident.

The I/I Function should be established as a General Staff Section when a criminal or terrorist act is involved. As the configuration of the ICS organization is flexible, the IC/UC may choose to combine these functions or create teams to perform these functions and may establish task force operations for crime scene processing. The nature and specifics of an incident, in addition to legal constraints, could restrict the type and scope of information that may be readily shared. When that information affects or threatens life safety of the responders and/or the public, the information can and should be shared with appropriate Command and General Staff.

Life safety is always the primary incident objective. The establishment of the I/I Function as a General Staff Section does not diminish or alter this primary objective in any way. It enhances the primacy of the life safety incident objective. For example, evidence recovered from the incident scene and the information produced from the intelligence/investigations activities may prevent a subsequent criminal or terrorist act from occurring at the incident site or at other locations.

Use and Organization of Groups

Under NIMS, Sections may be organized into Branches, Groups, and Divisions to meet the needs, scale, and complexity of an incident or event. If necessary to manage span of control, Divisions may be established as needed. The use of Branches is discussed in the next section.

Due to the functional nature of intelligence/investigations activities, Groups may be established representing specific mission areas. When applicable, the I/I Section Chief may create one or more Groups within the Section and designate a Group Supervisor for each Group. The Section Chief is expected to notify the Planning Section and, when applicable, Incident Command regarding the number of personnel assigned to the Section and to each Group. If any of the Groups are not used or have been deactivated, the Section Chief manages those responsibilities.

As permitted by local, state, tribal, territorial, insular area, and Federal law, Groups are used based on the needs of the incident. Groups that may be activated in the I/I Section include:

- **Investigative Operations Group:** Responsible for overall investigative effort
- **Intelligence Group:** Responsible for obtaining, analyzing, and managing unclassified, classified, and open source intelligence
- **Forensic Group:** Responsible for collection and integrity of physical evidence and the integrity of the crime scene
- **Missing Persons Group:** Responsible for directing the missing persons investigations and activities, as well as Family Assistance Center activities involving missing persons
- **Mass Fatality Management Group:** Responsible for directing the investigative/intelligence activities involving mass fatality management operations
- **Investigative Support Group:** Responsible for ensuring that required investigative personnel are made available expeditiously and that the necessary resources are properly distributed, maintained, safeguarded, stored, and returned, when appropriate.

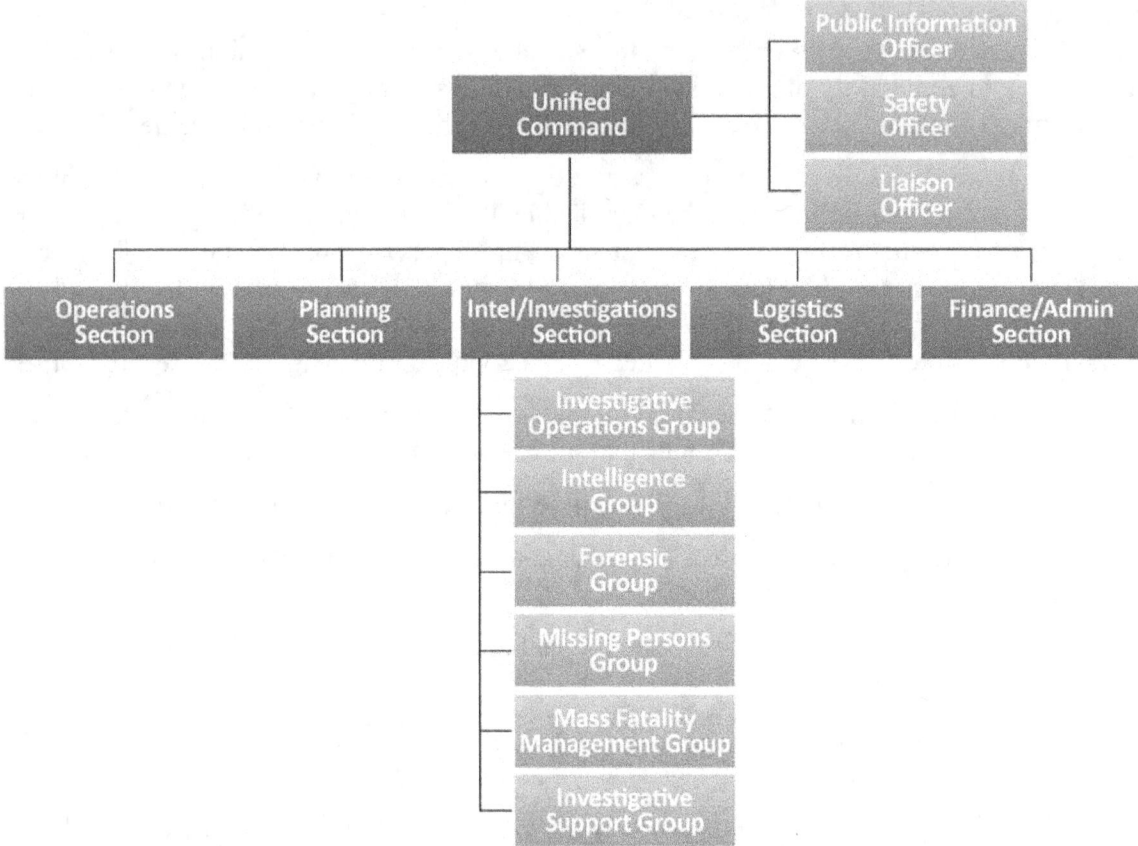

Figure 2: Intelligence/Investigations as a General Staff Section

The Groups are discussed further in the I/I FFOG.

Use and Organization of Branches

In specific instances, the work of the I/I Section may be performed by an extremely large number of personnel. Span of control problems due to a large number of personnel should be prevented or resolved (i.e., the Section is too large to support the direct reporting of Groups to the Section Chief). In this case or when other appropriate circumstances exist, the I/I Section Chief may activate one or more Branches within the I/I Section instead of one or more Groups and designate a Branch Director for each activated Branch. The Branches that may be activated are:

- Investigative Operations Branch
- Intelligence Branch
- Forensic Branch
- Missing Persons Branch
- Mass Fatality Management Branch
- Investigative Support Branch.

Summary

The I/I Function within ICS provides a flexible and scalable framework that allows for the integration of intelligence/investigations information and activities. The post-9/11 world requires an environment that supports the sharing of information across all levels of government, disciplines, and security domains. Situational awareness is enhanced by the I/I Function through the sharing of pre- and post-incident information, intelligence, and real-time incident intelligence and investigation activities. All entities involved in processing and sharing information should develop a common operating picture—both day-to-day and during an incident or planned event.

Intelligence/Investigations Function Field Operations Guide

The I/I FFOG assists those implementing the I/I Function as a Section within an incident command structure during incidents or planned events, regardless of type, cause, size, location, or complexity. The I/I FFOG describes the I/I Function as a General Staff Section to illustrate the potential tasks and responsibilities within the I/I Section.

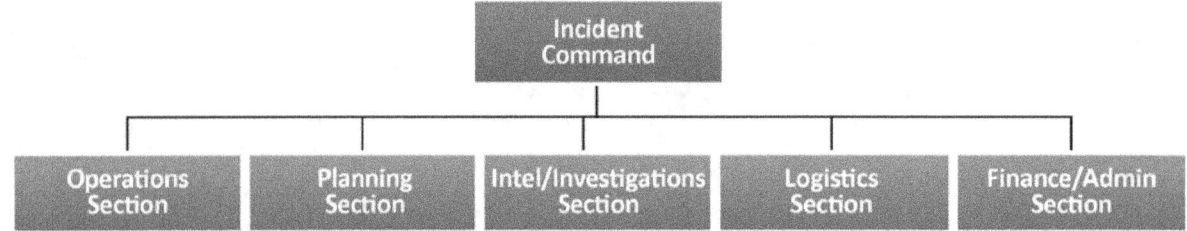

Figure 3: Intelligence/Investigations as a General Staff Section

The I/I FFOG does not replace emergency operations plans, laws, regulations, or ordinances. Rather, it provides guidance for personnel assigned to an incident or planned event. The information contained in the I/I FFOG supplements the user's experience, training, and knowledge in the performance of intelligence/investigations activities. It also provides a model for organizing and managing intelligence/investigations operations and activities.

The contents of this I/I FFOG are not a substitute for required formal training, intelligence/ investigations operations experience, and good judgment. Personnel using the I/I FFOG should have a comprehensive understanding of NIMS and ICS to ensure that they can effectively set up and operate an I/I Section. All agencies and jurisdictions should ensure that responders receive adequate and appropriate training to perform their assigned I/I Section duties and tasks.

Traditional law enforcement often uses the I/I Section to investigate incidents involving possible criminal or terrorist acts. However, many other investigative entities can use the I/I Function, including fire services (fire cause and origin), public health (disease outbreaks), medical examiner/coroner (mass fatality), the National Transportation Safety Board (transportation incidents), and the Environmental Protection Agency (oil spills). No matter what the nature or type of incident, personnel managing and performing intelligence/investigations activities must always comply with applicable statutes, case law, ordinances, regulations, and policies. Furthermore, the techniques they use must be authorized and lawful. Personnel managing and performing intelligence/investigations activities must realize that a violation of Federal, state, or local laws, regulations, or policies may have significant adverse consequences, including the suppression of critical evidence and personal civil liability.

The first part of the I/I FFOG provides an overview of the I/I Section as a whole and discusses aspects (e.g., setup, planning, logistics/communications, resource management, and coordination) that apply to the General Staff Section level of the I/I Function. The second part of the I/I FFOG provides more information on Groups and liaisons, coordination, and relevant task areas that can be set up under the I/I Section.

Intelligence/Investigations Functional Overview

The I/I FFOG describes the I/I Function when it is implemented as a General Staff Section equivalent to other Sections, such as Planning and Operations. The following section of the I/I FFOG addresses considerations relevant to the I/I Section as a whole (or to the Section Chief or Deputy Section Chief). Topics covered include steps and considerations for the initial setup of the I/I Section, the use of deputies, and internal and external relationships in three areas: planning, logistics, and resource management.

Initial Setup

The following is a list of suggested tasks and actions that the IC/UC and/or the potential I/I Section Chief may consider when initially establishing the I/I Section. Users of this guide are encouraged to tailor the list, adjusting it to reflect relevant laws, policies, regulations, and/or incident needs.

- Collect and evaluate information while responding to the incident scene.

- Obtain a comprehensive briefing regarding the incident.

- Confer with the IC/UC regarding how the I/I Section should be established and organized.

- Assume control regarding the I/I Section and ensure that incident personnel are promptly notified.

- Confer with the IC/UC to determine those intelligence/investigations agencies that are involved in the incident. The involvement of some agencies may be required by law.

- Ensure that:

  - Intelligence/investigations activities are expeditiously implemented. Intelligence/ Investigations activities may be initiated concurrently with life safety operations; absent extraordinary emergency circumstances, life safety operations incident objectives take priority over all other incident objectives

  - Required audio, data, image, and text communications equipment is obtained and communication procedures are implemented

  - A specific verbal or, if applicable, written I/I Section Communications Plan is prepared and provided to the Logistics Section

  - An Operations Section Technical Specialist is assigned to the I/I Section work area

  - An I/I Section Technical Specialist is assigned to the Operations Section work area

  - I/I Section staging areas are activated and a Staging Area Manager is designated for each staging area as needed

  - Resources that initially responded directly to the scene and resources that are subsequently requested are:

    o Immediately identified

    o Checked in

- o Briefed regarding the incident, particularly the intelligence/investigations aspects, and provided preliminary instructions, directions, information, data, precautions, requirements, etc.

- o Properly equipped

- o Wearing personal protective equipment (PPE)

- o Appropriately organized

- o Tracked

- o (If already on the scene) directed to continue performing the current assignments or reassigned to appropriate new assignments

- o (If not already on the scene) assigned to an initial assignment, directed to respond to a staging area, or directed to respond to an off-incident location

- Intelligence/investigations-related incident objectives, strategies, and priorities are formulated and documented.

- Confer with the Operations Section, Logistics Section, and Safety Officer regarding force protection, security, health, and safety issues.

- Establish an I/I Section work area at a secure location a reasonable distance from the Operations Section work area and the Incident Command Post (ICP).

- Frequently communicate and coordinate with all crime scenes, investigative scenes, and off-incident facilities regarding the investigation of the incident (e.g., hospital, local police department, state or major urban area fusion center, public health authorities, FBI Joint Operations Center, and others).

- When necessary, assign an I/I Section Technical Specialist to the ICP.

- Designate one or more Deputy I/I Section Chiefs.

- Activate one or more Groups or Branches.

- Request the necessary and appropriate intelligence and investigation resources and ensure that there is a controlled response of these resources.

- Establish and activate an "off-incident" I/I Operations Center facility or site; incident-related intelligence/investigations operations and activities can be managed and performed from this site to support and assist the I/I Section.

  - Designate an I/I Operations Center Director and provide a comprehensive briefing regarding the incident, particularly the intelligence/investigations aspects.

Use of Deputies

Depending on the size and scope of the incident, the I/I Section Chief may appoint a Deputy I/I Section Chief (or Chiefs). The following should be taken into consideration in the selection of this individual, in addition to some responsibilities that he or she might have as Deputy I/I Section Chief. It is important to remember that the use of Deputies is optional, according to the needs of the incident, as determined by the Section Chief.

Qualifications

The Deputy I/I Section Chief should:

- Have the same qualifications and experience as the I/I Section Chief
- Be capable of assuming the I/I Section Chief position permanently or temporarily when the Section Chief is absent.

Responsibilities

The role of the Deputy I/I Section Chief is flexible, and the Deputy I/I Section Chief may:

- Collect and analyze incident-related information and data
- Monitor and evaluate:
  - The current situation and estimate the potential future situation
  - The intelligence/investigations-related activities, resources, services, support, and reserves
  - The implementation and effectiveness of the documented intelligence/ investigations objectives, strategies, and priorities and the intelligence/investigations aspects of the IAP
- Monitor and assess:
  - The effectiveness of the I/I Section organizational structure
  - The performance of the I/I Section personnel and the I/I Operations Center Director and personnel
- Identify, evaluate, and resolve intelligence/investigations-related requirements and problems
- Maintain situational awareness for the I/I Section Chief
- Make important notifications (e.g., to the emergency operations center, local intelligence unit, state or major urban area fusion center, FBI Joint Operations Center, communications dispatcher, or similar coordination points)
- Participate in Planning Section meetings, when appropriate
- Perform specific activities and assignments as directed by the I/I Section Chief.

Selection of Deputies

One or more of the Deputy I/I Section Chiefs may be members of a different agency than the I/I Section Chief. Their member agency may be one that has:

- Legal jurisdiction or geographic responsibility for the incident scene
- Legal jurisdiction or geographic responsibility regarding the intelligence/investigations aspects of the incident
- Significant resources involved in the incident
- Been significantly affected by the incident.

Internal/External Intelligence/Investigations Activities and Relationships

Coordination is essential for effective and efficient management of any incident or planned event. When specialized resources, such as analysts or investigators, become active during an incident, the need for coordination increases, as other operational activities may conflict with intelligence/investigations activities.

This section describes three aspects of how the I/I Section can perform as a whole (i.e., planning, logistics, and resource management). It addresses the internal and external activities of each aspect to define the actions within the I/I Section, as well as how they relate to other Sections within the command structure.

In addition to the coordination requirements within the three aspects, there are several other steps an I/I Section Chief may take to ensure adequate communication both inside and outside the I/I Section. The I/I Section Chief may:

- Schedule and conduct:
  - Regular meetings and briefings with all of the Deputy I/I Section Chiefs, Group Supervisors, Managers, and Coordinators and with the I/I Operations Center Director to review current intelligence/investigations status and progress
  - Periodic meetings and briefings with all of the intelligence/ investigations personnel and I/I Operations Center personnel
- Establish and maintain liaison and integrated operations with all levels and functions within the incident management organization while adhering to the established chain of command and the ICS protocols
- Until all relevant intelligence/investigations activities have been completed, confer with the Command and General Staffs to ensure that procedures are implemented to prevent:
  - Interference with intelligence/investigations activities
  - Disturbance of known or suspected crime scenes or investigative scenes
  - Disturbance of decedent
- Frequently communicate and coordinate with the Operations Section regarding tactical intelligence/investigations-related activities (e.g., warrant executions, arrests, searches, seizures, physical surveillance, electronic surveillance, stops/detentions, directed enforcement operations, undercover officer operations, identification activities, and epidemiological surveillance), and involve the respective legal authorities (e.g., prosecutors' office, magistrates, and courts of jurisdiction) as required
- Confer with the Command and General Staffs to ensure that all I/I Section activity is continually coordinated
- Confer with the Liaison Officer to ensure that I/I Section activity is coordinated with the appropriate governmental agencies, nongovernmental organizations, and the private sector, including communicating through appropriate channels to the U.S. Intelligence Community, as well as, the law enforcement, homeland security, military, and international security/liaison communities

- Ensure that the Public Information Officer assists with public affairs and media-related activities

- Coordinate with the Public Information Officer to ensure that public information-related activities do not violate or contravene operations security, operational security, or information security procedures.

Planning

Coordinated planning is a keystone of both NIMS and ICS. How Sections plan together can play a large role in determining the degree of success in response operations, including those related to intelligence/investigations activities. In particular, staff responsible for I/I Section planning should not allow intelligence/investigations-related incident objectives to conflict with overall incident strategies and objectives. In instances where a conflict may arise, Sections must deconflict those issues prior to engaging in actions that could compromise the incident objectives or endanger personnel. The following tasks and responsibilities relate to both the internal and external planning efforts of the I/I Section.

Internal Tasks/Responsibilities

- Analyze incident or planned event-related information and data, evaluate the current situation, and estimate the potential future situation.

- Maximize situational awareness and develop an accurate common operating picture.

- Ensure that:

  - Required resources, reserves, services, and support are identified and requested in the appropriate manner

  - Problems, requirements, issues, and concerns are identified and resolved

  - Intelligence/investigations incident objectives and strategies are formulated and documented

  - All of the intelligence/investigations aspects and components of the IAP and the Demobilization Plan are implemented.

External Tasks/Responsibilities

- Participate in Planning Section meetings.

- Assist in:

  - Reviewing incident priorities and establishing incident objectives

  - Formulation and preparation of the IAP and provide, as applicable, I/I Section organization chart, supporting plan, and supporting materials/attachments (e.g., maps, data, images, matrices, briefings, situation reports, and assessments).

- Confer with the Planning Section regarding:

  - Planning functions and activities

  - The intelligence/investigations aspects and components of the IAP, including incident objectives, strategies, and priorities; information on resources, reserves, services, and support; operations; and activities

- The intelligence/investigations aspects and components of the Demobilization Plan
- Documentation and records management procedures, measures, and activities.

- Ensure that:
  - Intelligence/investigations needs are considered when the incident objectives and strategies are formulated and the IAP is developed
  - Activities related to the formulation, documentation, and dissemination of the IAP and other planning activities do not violate operations security, operational security, or information security procedures, measures, or activities.

Logistics/Communications

Incidents that warrant the establishment of an I/I Section often require provisions for secure or other special communications capabilities. The following tasks and responsibilities relate to both the internal and external logistics/communications efforts of the I/I Section.

Internal Tasks/Responsibilities

- Ensure that:
  - Audio, data, image, and text communications procedures, measures, and activities are implemented
  - A verbal or written I/I Section Communications Plan is prepared
  - All intelligence/investigations personnel are familiar with life safety warning communications protocols used by other response organizations for imminent life-threatening situations.
- Prepare and implement an incident-specific Communications Plan as necessary, particularly if secure communications systems or security protocols are appropriate (including communications mechanisms used to convey critical information).
- When necessary:
  - Designate I/I Section primary and secondary system radio channels and primary and secondary point-to-point radio channels
  - Ensure that a sufficient number of communications devices are obtained, including secure communications devices (e.g., secure telephone unit, secure telephone equipment, mobile Sensitive Compartmented Information Facility [SCIF], and secure video teleconference system).

External Tasks/Responsibilities

- Confer with the Logistics Section (Communications Unit Leader) regarding communications systems, guidelines, constraints, and protocols.
- Coordinate with the Logistics Section regarding the preparation of the intelligence/ investigations component of the Communications Plan.
- Ensure that audio, data, image, and text communications procedures, measures, and activities are implemented throughout the command structure to facilitate the communication of classified information, sensitive compartmented information, and sensitive information.

Resource Management

Intelligence/Investigations often require specialized equipment and trained personnel resources that may or may not be suited for inclusion with other incident resources. Specialized resources may require added security and confidentiality. Therefore, the I/I Section should coordinate with the Logistics Section and other Command Staff to ensure that adequate resource management processes are in place. The following tasks and responsibilities relate to both the internal and external resource management efforts of the I/I Section.

Internal Tasks/Responsibilities

- Evaluate the current situation, estimate the potential future situation, determine the resource needs for one or more operational periods, and request the necessary operational and support resources (e.g., personnel, equipment, or vehicles).

- Maintain control of requested resources and ensure that requested resources do not deploy directly to the incident scene. (Follow standard ICS protocols for mobilization, dispatch, deployment, check-in, and task assignments.)

- Ensure that I/I Section staging areas are activated and a Staging Area Manager is designated for each of the activated staging areas as needed.

External Tasks/Responsibilities

- Confer with the Command and General Staffs to identify anticipated intelligence/investigations resource needs.

- Confer with the Planning Section and Logistics Section and, if necessary, the Liaison Officer regarding resource-related activities.

- Ensure that resources that initially responded directly to the scene and resources that are subsequently requested are:
  - Immediately identified
  - Checked in (authorized for on-scene activities)
  - Briefed regarding the incident, particularly the intelligence/investigations aspects, and provided preliminary instructions, directions, information, data, precautions, requirements; all such briefings must be made consistent with legal requirements for the protection of information, including but not limited to limiting the distribution of classified information to those with proper clearances and the need to know
  - Equipped
  - Wearing PPE for the known or suspected threat or hazard
  - Organized consistent with ICS protocols
  - Tracked
  - (If already on the scene) directed to continue performing the current assignments or reassigned to appropriate new assignments
  - (If not already on the scene) assigned to an initial assignment, directed to respond to a staging area, or directed to respond to an "off-incident" location.

Intelligence/Investigations Physical Location and Work Area

There are unique considerations for the physical location of the I/I Section in relation to the ICP and other General Staff Sections. This is a result of both the sensitive nature of intelligence/investigations operations and the need for consistent communication with the other portions of the command structure. The I/I Section work area is the location where the I/I Section Chief and appropriate staff remains, as well as manages, coordinates, and directs all of the intelligence/investigations operations, functions, and activities.

Considerations to remember as the I/I Section work area location is being selected and maintained include:

- Establishing the I/I Section work area at a secure location a reasonable distance from the Operations Section work area and the ICP
  - The I/I Section work area may be any type of appropriate building, structure, vehicle, or area that is available (e.g., automobile, van, trailer, tent, or room in a building)
- In coordination with the Logistics Section, choosing a location that:
  - Is sufficiently large
  - Is a reasonable and appropriate distance from the incident scene
  - Provides safety, health, security, and force protection
  - Provides easy and expeditious access and egress
  - Provides adequate workspace
  - Allows for expansion
  - Permits continuous operations
  - Provides adequate utilities, wireline and wireless communication services, sanitation, and other essential infrastructure and services
- Conferring with the Operations Section, Logistics Section, and Safety Officer to ensure that adequate safety, health, security, and force protection measures are implemented in the I/I Section work area
- When necessary, ensuring that:
  - The location where the I/I Section work area is situated has been searched for any force protection/security hazards, health hazards, and safety hazards
  - There are personnel to provide force protection/security regarding non-hostile unauthorized persons; persons conducting intelligence collection, surveillance, or reconnaissance activities/operations; hostile persons; emotionally disturbed persons, etc.
  - Identification, access/entry control, and badging procedures, measures, functions, and activities are implemented.

Groups and Structure within the Intelligence/Investigations Section

The I/I Section Chief has the option of creating one or more Groups to oversee the activities of the Section. Groups that may be activated in the I/I Section are discussed below.

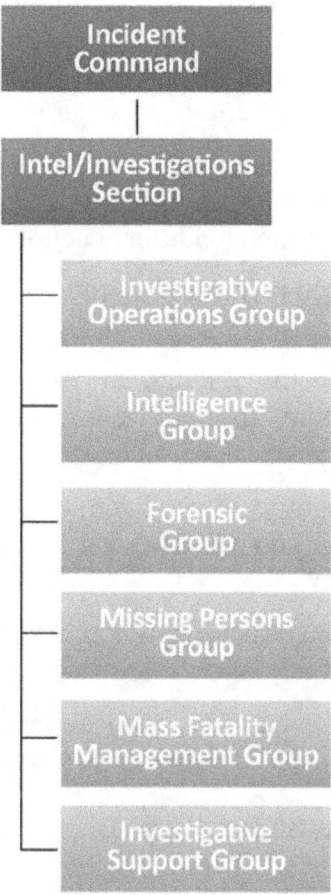

Figure 4: Intelligence/Investigations Section Organization

Investigative Operations Group

The Investigative Operations Group is the primary Group in the I/I Section. It manages and directs the overall investigative effort. The Investigative Operations Group uses the information that all of the other Groups and the I/I Operations Center produce to accomplish the mission of the I/I Section. The primary case investigator and primary supervisor are assigned to the Investigative Operations Group.

The Investigative Operations Group ensures that:

- An intelligence/investigations plan is developed and implemented

- Each investigative lead/task is recorded in the assignment log or database and is assigned to appropriate personnel in the proper priority order and sequence

- Each assigned investigative lead/task is properly, completely, and expeditiously performed

- Results of each assigned investigative lead/task are documented and all of the associated materials are invoiced, safeguarded, and examined

- All forensic evidence, digital and multimedia evidence, and investigative evidence (e.g., documents, images, audios, and data) are invoiced, safeguarded, and analyzed

- All investigative reports and materials associated with the results of each assigned investigative lead/task and the related forensic, investigative, and digital and multimedia evidence are discussed with authorized personnel; reports, materials, and evidence should also be examined and evaluated to determine whether the assigned investigative lead/task was properly performed

- Each examined and evaluated investigative lead/task is categorized as closed (no further action or new leads generated) or open (additional action required)

- Information regarding each closed investigative lead/task is recorded in the assignment log or database

- Results of each assigned investigative lead/task are exploited and, if applicable, one or more subsequent additional follow-up investigative leads/tasks are identified, recorded, assigned, performed, etc.

- A chronological record of the significant intelligence/investigations information, activities, decisions, directives, and results is documented and, if appropriate, displayed on situation boards or a Web log

- Intelligence/Investigations techniques and tactics are used in the proper priority order and sequence

- Required legal advice, services, documents, applications, and process are obtained

- Documentation and records management procedures are implemented

- The Intelligence Group examines and analyzes all unassigned, assigned, and completed investigative leads/tasks

- The I/I Operations Center and all of the Groups are communicating and coordinating with the Investigative Operations Group

- There is communication and coordination with a designated investigative supervisor or investigator assigned to each of the crime scenes and each of the significantly involved investigative scenes, hospitals, and off-incident facilities.

The Investigative Operations Group uses techniques and tactics including, but not limited to:

- Nontechnical and technical canvasses

- Interviews and interrogations

- Prisoner debriefings

- Identification procedures

- Searches and seizures

- Database/Record queries

- Electronic communication (e.g., telephone, computer) investigative records acquisition and analysis

- Physical surveillance

- Electronic surveillance

- Acquisition and analysis of records and other evidence

- Polygraph examinations

- Undercover officer and confidential informant operations

- Activation and use of tiplines, hotlines, and/or call centers

- Dissemination of alarms, "Be on the Lookout" messages, alerts, warnings, and notices

- Obtaining and securing of sources of investigatory data, such as flight data recorders, cockpit voice recorders, vehicle electronic data recorders, radar data, and 9-1-1 tapes.

Depending upon the scope, complexity, and size of the I/I Section, the Investigative Operations Group Supervisor may activate one or more of the positions below. As the configuration of the ICS organization is flexible, the IC/UC may choose to combine these positions or create teams to perform the following functions:

- Assignment Manager

- Recorder

- Evidence Manager

- Physical Surveillance Coordinator

- Electronic Surveillance Coordinator

- Electronic Communication Records Coordinator

- Tactical Operations Coordinator.

Intelligence Group

The Intelligence Group is responsible for three major functions: (1) information intake and assessment; (2) operations security, operational security, and information security; and (3) information/intelligence management.

The information intake and assessment function ensures that incoming information, except the results of investigative leads/tasks, is:

- Communicated directly to the Intelligence Group

- Documented on an information control form and/or entered into an information control database

- Evaluated to determine the correct information security designation (e.g., classified or sensitive) and the required information security procedures

- Initially evaluated and categorized as being information that:

  - May require the Investigative Operations Group to assign an investigative lead/task (this information is communicated to the Investigative Operations Group for final determination regarding whether an investigative lead/task is assigned)

  - Constitutes intelligence but does not require the Investigative Operations Group to assign an investigative lead/task (absent unusual circumstances, this information is communicated to the Investigative Operations Group)

- Assessed by performing the appropriate databases/records queries

- Analyzed to determine whether the incoming information is related to any existing information

- Disseminated to I/I Section and I/I Operations Center personnel.

Operations security, operational security, and information security activities include, but are not limited to:

- Ensuring that:

  - Operations security, operational security, and information security procedures and activities are implemented

  - Classified information is disseminated to personnel who have the required clearance, access, and "need to know" and is disseminated in compliance with all associated "caveats"

  - Sensitive information is disseminated to authorized personnel who have the required need to know and in strict compliance with applicable restrictions and laws

- Maintaining liaison through appropriate channels with the Intelligence Community, the intelligence components of other agencies affected by the incident, and the fusion centers

- Conferring with the Command and General Staffs to ensure that the confidentiality and security of intelligence/investigations activities are not compromised.

The information/intelligence management function activities include, but are not limited to:

- Ensuring that:

  - Tactical and strategic intelligence/investigations information is collected using appropriate, authorized, and lawful techniques and activities

  - Intelligence requirements are used to manage and direct intelligence collection efforts

  - Database and record queries are performed

  - Language translation and deciphering and decryption services are provided

  - Intelligence/investigations information is documented, secured, organized, evaluated, collated, processed, exploited, and analyzed

  - Intelligence information needs, requests for intelligence, intelligence gaps, and standing and ad hoc intelligence requirements are identified, documented, analyzed, validated, produced (if applicable), and resolved

  - Requests for intelligence/investigations information are made to the appropriate governmental agencies, nongovernmental organizations, private sector entities/individuals, the media, and the public

  - Finished and, if appropriate, raw intelligence/investigations information is documented and produced as needed (e.g., records, data, warnings, situation reports, briefings, bulletins, and/or assessments)

  - Unclassified or lesser classified tearline reports are produced regarding appropriate classified information

- Classified information and/or access-controlled sensitive compartmented information and/or caveated/restricted information is sanitized to use the information to create and investigate leads/tasks, publish intelligence products, prepare warrant applications and accusatory instruments, etc.

- Intelligence/investigations information, documents, requirements, and products are appropriately disseminated

- Threat information/intelligence is immediately transmitted to the IC/UC, the Operations Section Chief, and, if necessary, other authorized personnel

- Notifying and conferring with subject matter experts

- Identifying and collecting intelligence/investigations information

- When applicable, ensuring that requests for intelligence/investigations information are documented, analyzed, managed, and resolved

- Conferring with the Planning Section regarding information/intelligence-related activities as needed.

Depending upon the size, complexity, and scope of the I/I Section, the Intelligence Group Supervisor may activate one or more of the following positions:

- Information Intake and Assessment Manager

- Requirements Coordinator

- Collection Coordinator

- Processing and Exploitation Coordinator

- Analysis and Production Coordinator

- Dissemination Coordinator

- Critical Infrastructure and Key Resources Protection Coordinator

- Classified National Security Information Security Officer

- Requests for Information Coordinator.

As the configuration of the ICS organization is flexible, the IC/UC may choose to combine these functions or create teams to perform these functions.

Forensic Group

The Forensic Group is responsible for managing crime scenes and directing the processing of the forensic evidence, digital and multimedia evidence, and decedents. The Forensic Group also ensures that the proper types of examinations, analyses, comparisons, and enhancements are performed on the forensic evidence, digital and multimedia evidence and decedents in the proper sequence by the appropriate laboratories, analytical service providers, and morgues. The Forensic Group coordinates with the Mass Fatality Management Group and the medical examiner/coroner on matters related to the examination, recovery, and movement of decedents.

The Forensic Group is responsible for ensuring that:

- The number of crime scenes and decedents, and the location of each of the crime scenes and decedents, are expeditiously and properly determined

- The size, configuration, boundaries, etc., of each of the crime scenes are properly determined and each of the crime scenes is sufficiently large

- Each of the crime scenes and decedents is secured and safeguarded and access to each of the crime scenes and decedents is controlled, restricted, and limited

- The prevention of contamination, alteration, loss, destruction, etc., of forensic, digital, and multimedia evidence and decedents

- The documentation of the rank/title, name, command/unit, agency, tax/employee identification number, etc., of each person who enters a crime scene and/or touches, searches, disturbs, moves, etc., decedents

- Personnel processing crime scenes and decedents confer with the primary case investigator, the primary case supervisor, medical examiner/coroner, and other appropriate personnel

- Each of the crime scenes and decedents is expeditiously processed in an appropriate manner and in the proper priority order and sequence

- Forensic evidence, digital and multimedia evidence, and decedents are expeditiously and appropriately delivered to one or more suitable laboratories, analytical service providers, and/or morgue facilities

- The receiving laboratory, analytical service provider, and/or morgue examines, analyzes, and compares forensic evidence, digital and multimedia evidence, and decedents in priority order; the Forensic Group also ensures that the proper number and types of examinations, analyses, comparisons, etc., are performed in the proper sequence

- Personnel processing crime scenes and decedents, the primary case investigator, and the primary case supervisor confer with the appropriate laboratory, analytical service provider, and morgue personnel

- Forensic evidence, digital and multimedia evidence, and decedents are delivered to a designated facility or site at an appropriate time for storage, secured, retained, and disposed of in a proper manner at an appropriate time

- When necessary, bomb squad assessment and render-safe activities are implemented

- When necessary, forensic debris and post-blast crime scene activities are implemented

- Crime scene reconstruction techniques and subject matter experts are used as needed

- Records and reports are prepared regarding forensic evidence, digital and multimedia evidence, and decedents

- Crime scenes, including decedents located at the crime scenes, are not prematurely released.

Depending upon the size, complexity, and scope of the I/I Section, the Forensic Group Supervisor may activate one or more of the following positions:

- Crime Scene Coordinator

- Bomb Operations Coordinator

- Chemical, Biological, Radiological, Nuclear/Hazardous Materials Evidence Coordinator

- Forensic Evidence Analysis Manager (including digital and multimedia evidence).

Missing Persons Group

The Missing Persons Group directs missing persons operations and activities, as well as Family Assistance Center activities involving missing persons. The Missing Persons Group is responsible for ensuring that:

- Missing persons information reporting, documentation, security, assessment, categorization, consolidation, tracking, storage, dissemination, etc., activities are implemented

- In communication and coordination with the Public Information Officer, authorized information and instructions regarding the proper procedures for reporting missing persons information are disseminated to the media, the public, governmental agencies, nongovernmental organizations, and private entities/individuals

- Each of the reported actual missing persons is located, the related required notifications are made in an appropriate and timely manner to the appropriate persons, and the required information is documented in an appropriate manner

- Appropriate documentation of the required information regarding the number of reported:

  - Potential missing persons

  - Actual missing persons

  - Actual missing persons located

- Required information; data; records; images; DNA reference samples; investigative evidence; forensic evidence; digital and multimedia evidence; and non-evidence property regarding missing persons are obtained at one or more Family Assistance Centers and/or appropriate facilities/areas.

Depending upon the size, complexity, and scope of the I/I Section, the Missing Persons Group Supervisor may activate one or more of the following positions:

- Missing Persons Coordinator

- Family Assistance Center Coordinator.

As the configuration of the ICS organization is flexible, the IC/UC may choose to combine these functions or create teams to perform these functions.

The Missing Persons Group Supervisor is responsible for ensuring that coordination and information sharing are established with the Forensic Group, the Mass Fatality Management Group, the medical examiner/coroner, and the Mass Fatality Branch in the Operations Section, when activated.

Mass Fatality Management Group

The Mass Fatality Management Group will direct intelligence/investigations activities involving mass fatality management operations. This includes the intelligence/investigations-related Family Assistance Center activities involving decedents and unidentified persons.

The Mass Fatality Management Group is responsible for ensuring that:

- Mass fatality management operations and activities are implemented

- Decedent information reporting, documentation, security, assessment, categorization, consolidation, tracking, storage, dissemination, etc., activities are implemented

- When necessary, Disaster Mortuary Operational Response Teams or other similar resources are requested

- When necessary, debris sifting operations are implemented

- All of the decedents are identified; related required notifications are made in an appropriate and timely manner to the appropriate persons; and the required information is documented in an appropriate manner

- Mass fatality-related public health hazards are mitigated

- The medical examiner/coroner expeditiously determines the cause and manner of death of each of the decedents and the final disposition of each of the decedents

- The appropriate authority expeditiously issues a death certificate regarding each of the decedents

- Required information, data, records, images, DNA reference samples, investigative evidence, forensic evidence, digital/multimedia evidence, and non-evidence property regarding decedents are obtained at one or more Family Assistance Centers and/or appropriate facilities/areas.

Depending upon the size, complexity, and scope of the I/I Section, the Mass Fatality Management Group Supervisor may activate one or more of the following positions:

- Mass Fatality Management Coordinator

- Field Site/Recovery Coordinator

- Morgue/Postmortem Examinations Coordinator

- Victim Identification Coordinator

- Family Assistance Center Coordinator

- Quality Assurance Coordinator.

As the configuration of the ICS organization is flexible, the IC/UC may choose to combine these functions or create teams to perform these functions.

The Mass Fatality Management Group Supervisor is responsible for ensuring that coordination and information sharing are established between the Missing Persons Group and the Forensic Group.

Investigative Support Group

The I/I Section may require the use of specialized operational and support resources. The Investigative Support Group works closely with the Command and General Staffs, particularly the Logistics Section and Planning Section, to ensure that necessary resources, services, and support are obtained for the I/I Section.

The Investigative Support Group is responsible for ensuring that:

- I/I Section staging areas are activated and each staging area is situated at an appropriate location; a Staging Area Manager is designated for each of the activated staging areas

- Personnel, equipment, vehicles, aircraft, watercraft, supplies, facilities, infrastructure, networks, and other operational and support resources are expeditiously ordered and obtained

- Food and beverages are provided to personnel as needed

- Technical and nontechnical services and support are expeditiously ordered and obtained

- Resources, services, and support that must be procured are identified, ordered, and obtained in a timely manner

- Resources are maintained, repaired or replaced when necessary, safeguarded, tracked, documented, properly used, and retrieved

- Accountability procedures and activities are implemented for operational and support resources

- Resources are recovered and/or demobilized when no longer needed

- Records and reports are prepared regarding investigative support-related activities.

Depending upon the size, complexity, and scope of the I/I Section, the Investigative Support Group Supervisor may activate one or more of the following positions:

- One or More Staging Area Managers

  - Properly document information regarding responding resources.

  - Categorize and separate responding personnel based upon one or more of the following criteria:

    o Agency jurisdiction and legal authority

    o Personnel technical skills

    o Personnel nontechnical skills

    o Personnel clearance and access

    o Personnel proficiency.

  - Ensure that:

    o Personnel resources are properly credentialed

    o Identification, access/entry control, and badging procedures and measures are implemented

    o Personnel resources are equipped and wearing required PPE

    o Personnel resources are organized

    o Personnel resources receive a briefing regarding the incident, particularly the intelligence/investigations aspects, and are provided preliminary instructions, directions, information, data, precautions, and requirements

    o Personnel resources are deployed and assigned or are directed to remain as reserves

- o Resources are tracked.
- ▪ Intelligence/Investigations Section Work Area Manager
  - • Ensure that the I/I Section work area is maintained in an orderly manner.
  - • In coordination with the Logistics Section, ensure that all of the utilities, wireline and wireless communication services, sanitation, accommodations, infrastructure, and other essential services and support-related requirements are satisfied.
- ▪ Resource Coordinator
  - • If a significant number of intelligence/investigations resources are required, work directly with counterparts in the Logistics Section to order the resources and in the Planning Section to account for all resources.
  - • Ensure that:
    - o Technical and nontechnical services and support are expeditiously ordered and obtained
    - o Resources, services, and support that must be procured are identified, ordered, and obtained in a timely manner
    - o Resources are maintained, repaired or replaced when necessary; safeguarded; tracked; documented; properly used; and retrieved
    - o Accountability procedures and activities are implemented regarding operational and support resources
    - o Resources are recovered and/or demobilized when no longer needed.
- ▪ Communications Coordinator
  - • This position works directly with the Logistics Section.
  - • Ensure that:
    - o Audio, data, image, and text communications procedures and activities are implemented
    - o A sufficient number of communication devices, including secure communication devices, are obtained, maintained, repaired or replaced when necessary, safeguarded, appropriately distributed, tracked, documented, properly used, and retrieved.
    - o Radio channels are monitored at the I/I Section work area
    - o The I/I Section Communications Plan is prepared and updated and is communicated to the Logistics Section.
  - • Ascertain the designated "system" radio channels and "point-to-point" radio channels that are being used for the incident.
  - • Designate the I/I Section "system" radio channels and "point-to-point" radio channels as needed.

- Physical Security Coordinator
  - This position ensures that adequate physical security measures are in place (but does not have authority to implement site security actions).
  - Confer with the Operations Section, Logistics Section, and Safety Officer regarding personnel safety plans, procedures, and activities.
  - Ensure that:
    - All of the involved areas are searched for force protection and security, health, safety, and environmental hazards
    - All force protection and security, health, safety, and environmental hazards are identified, addressed, and resolved
    - All dangerous or hazardous people, weapons, devices, objects, animals, and conditions are identified, isolated, controlled, and safely mitigated
    - Actual and/or potential threats are identified, investigated, and resolved
    - Identification, access/entry control, and badging procedures and measures are implemented
    - Personnel safety procedures and measures are implemented regarding the I/I Section work area.

As the configuration of the ICS organization is flexible, the IC/UC may choose to combine these functions or create teams to perform these functions.

List of Abbreviations and Glossary of Key Terms

List of Abbreviations

EMR–ISAC	Emergency Management and Response–Information Sharing and Analysis Center
FBI	Federal Bureau of Investigation
HSIN	Homeland Security Information Network
I/I	Intelligence/Investigations
I/I FFOG	Intelligence/Investigations Function Field Operations Guide
IAP	Incident Action Plan
IC	Incident Commander
ICP	Incident Command Post
ICS	Incident Command System
LEO	Law Enforcement Online
NIMS	National Incident Management System
PPD	Presidential Policy Directive
PPE	Personal Protective Equipment
RISS	Regional Intelligence Sharing Systems
SCI	Sensitive Compartmented Information
SCIF	Sensitive Compartment Information Facility
UC	Unified Command

Glossary of Key Terms

Analysis: The comprehensive and systematic examination, assessment, and evaluation of collected, processed, and exploited information/intelligence to identify significant facts, ascertain trends and patterns, develop alternative options, forecast future events, and derive valid conclusions.

Branch: The organizational level having functional or geographical responsibility for major aspects of incident operations. A Branch is organizationally situated between the Section Chief and the Division or Group in the Operations Section and between the Section and Units in the Logistics Section.

Caveat: A prohibition regarding the dissemination, sharing, distribution, or delivery of information/intelligence. Dissemination caveats are not a level of classification but are used in conjunction with the appropriate classification level. The following are examples of dissemination caveats:

- ORCON (Dissemination and Extraction of Information Controlled by Originator): No further dissemination can occur without the prior approval of the originating entity that provided the subject information/intelligence

- NOFORN (Not Releasable to Foreign Nationals): May not be provided in any form to foreign governments, international organizations, coalition partners, foreign nationals, or immigrant aliens

- REL TO: Authorized for release to (specify one or more countries)

- RELIDO: Releasable by Information Disclosure Officer.

Classified National Security Information (also referred to as "Classified Information"): Any data, file, paper, record, or computer screen containing information associated with the national defense or foreign relations of the United States and bearing the markings Confidential, Secret, or Top Secret. This information has been determined pursuant to Executive Order 13526 or any predecessor order to require protection against unauthorized disclosure and is marked (Confidential, Secret, or Top Secret) to indicate its classified status. There are three levels of classified information:

- Confidential: Applied to information, the unauthorized disclosure of which reasonably could be expected to cause damage to the national security that the original classification authority is able to identify or describe

- Secret: Applied to information, the unauthorized disclosure of which reasonably could be expected to cause serious damage to the national security that the original classification authority is able to identify or describe

- Top Secret: Applied to information, the unauthorized disclosure of which reasonably could be expected to cause exceptionally grave damage to the national security that the original classification authority is able to identify or describe.

Collection: The gathering of information through approved techniques to address and/or resolve intelligence requirements. The sources of information that are used during the Collection step of the Intelligence Cycle include Human Intelligence, Signals Intelligence, Imagery Intelligence, Open Source Intelligence, and Measurement and Signature Intelligence.

Command Staff: The staff that reports directly to the Incident Commander, including the Public Information Officer, Safety Officer, Liaison Officer, and other positions as required. They may have an assistant or assistants, as needed.

Coroner: The official, in coroner jurisdictions, charged with the medicolegal investigation of deaths and fatality management. This individual is responsible for certifying the identification and determining the cause and manner of death of deceased persons and decedents. This individual has statutory jurisdiction over all bodies and decedents falling within the geographic jurisdiction and within certain prescribed categories of death. Mass fatality incidents may involve victims who are within those statutorily prescribed categories.

Crime Scene: An area or areas that contain physical evidence and/or decedents that may have forensic, investigative, digital and multimedia, demonstrative, or other probative value. Crime scenes include casualty collection areas and fatality collection points.

Critical Infrastructure: Assets, systems, and networks, whether physical or virtual, so vital to the United States that the incapacitation or destruction of such assets, systems, or networks would have a debilitating impact on security, national economic security, national public health or safety, or any combination of those matters.

Decedents: Any body or portion thereof that is clinically deceased. Decedents include whole bodies, body parts, and body fragments including unassociated tissue.

Deconfliction: The avoidance of duplication or interference.

Digital Evidence: Physical evidence consisting of information of probative value that is stored or transmitted in binary form.

Digital and Multimedia Evidence: Electronic physical evidence that does or may require scientific examination, analysis, comparison, and/or enhancement. Digital and multimedia evidence includes electronic text, data, audio, and image evidence, such as video, closed-circuit television, photograph, camera, computer, radio, personal information management device, wireline telephone, wireless telephone, smart phone, satellite telephone, Wi-Fi messaging device, digital multimedia device, pager, navigational system/global positioning system, storage device or media, server, network device, wireless device, modem, antenna, peripheral device, telephone caller identification device, audio recording device, answering machine, and facsimile machine.

Director of National Intelligence: Position created pursuant to the Intelligence Reform Act of 2004. The Director of National Intelligence has "executive authority" to oversee the U.S. Intelligence Community.

Family Assistance Center: An entity that facilitates the exchange of information between disaster responders and the family members and friends of those injured, missing, unidentified, or identified as deceased. One function performed in the Family Assistance Center is the gathering of ante mortem medical and dental records of possible missing persons. Family Assistance Center personnel address the immediate emotional needs of the victims' families and friends and provide accurate and timely information in an appropriate setting. The Family Assistance Center should also address the basic physical needs of these family members and friends of victims, including food, shelter, transportation, Internet access, telephone, childcare, language translation, disaster mental health services, and emergency medical services, if necessary.

Force Protection and Security: Protecting responders from hazards involving one or more persons, weapons, devices, objects, animals, conditions, or situations.

Forensic Evidence: Non-electronic physical evidence that does or may require scientific examination, analysis, comparison, and/or enhancement.

Forensics: The use of science and technology to investigate and establish facts in criminal or civil courts of law.

General Staff: A group of incident management personnel organized according to function and reporting to the Incident Commander. The General Staff normally consists of the Operations Section Chief, Planning Section Chief, Logistics Section Chief, and Finance/Administration Section Chief. An Intelligence/Investigations Section Chief may be designated, if required, to meet incident management needs.

Group: An organizational subdivision established to divide the incident management structure into functional areas of operation. Groups are composed of resources assembled to perform a special function not necessarily within a single geographic division.

Human Intelligence: Intelligence information acquired by human sources through covert and overt collection techniques.

Imagery Intelligence: The collection, analysis, and interpretation of conventional, analog, and digital image information/data.

Incident Action Plan: An oral or written plan containing general objectives reflecting the overall strategy for managing an incident. The Incident Action Plan may include the identification of operational resources and assignments. It may also include attachments that provide direction and important information for management of the incident during one or more operational periods.

Incident Command Post: The field location where the primary functions are performed. The Incident Command Post may be co-located with the Incident Base or other incident facilities.

Incident Objectives: Statements of guidance and direction needed to select appropriate strategies and the tactical direction of resources. Incident objectives are based on realistic expectations of what can be accomplished when all allocated resources have been effectively deployed. Incident objectives should be achievable and measurable, yet flexible enough to allow strategic and tactical alternatives.

Information Security: The policies, practices, and procedures that ensure that information/intelligence stored, processed, transmitted, etc., using information technology systems and networks is secure, and not vulnerable to inappropriate or unauthorized discovery, access, export, use, modification, etc.

Intelligence: Generally speaking, information that has been evaluated and from which conclusions have been drawn to make informed decisions. Intelligence can be defined slightly differently depending on the agency or organization of focus. Types of intelligence include:

- Raw Intelligence: Unevaluated collected information/intelligence, usually from a single source, that has not been fully processed, exploited, integrated, evaluated, analyzed, and interpreted

- Finished Intelligence: The product, usually from multiple sources, resulting from the processing, exploitation, integration, evaluation, analysis, and interpretation of collected information/intelligence that fully addresses an issue or threat based upon available information/intelligence

- Strategic Intelligence: Information tailored to support the planning and execution of agency-wide intelligence and investigative programs, and the development of long-term policies, plans, and strategies

- Tactical Intelligence: Information that directly supports ongoing operations and investigations.

Intelligence Gap: An unanswered question regarding a criminal, cyber, or national security issue or threat.

Intelligence Information Need: The information/intelligence needed to eliminate one or more intelligence gaps and/or to support the mission of the governmental agency, nongovernmental organization, or private entity/individual submitting the intelligence information need.

Intelligence Information Report: The standard product used to document "raw" information/intelligence and to disseminate the "raw" information/intelligence to national policymakers, the U.S. Intelligence Community, the Homeland Security Community, and the

Law Enforcement Community. Analysts use Intelligence Information Reports and other available sources of information/intelligence to produce "finished" information/intelligence.

Intelligence/Investigations Operations Center: Intelligence/Investigations activities are managed and performed at the Intelligence/Investigations Operations Center to support and assist the Intelligence/Investigations Section. Furthermore, if intelligence/investigations activities continue after the incident and resources at the incident site have been demobilized, the investigation may be managed exclusively at the Intelligence/Investigations Operations Center.

Intelligence Requirement: The information and/or intelligence that must be collected and produced to eliminate intelligence gaps. Intelligence requirements convert intelligence gaps and the associated intelligence information needs into specific instructions regarding what information and/or intelligence to collect, report, produce, and disseminate. Intelligence requirements provide the questions that are asked of Human Intelligence sources and the information that is sought from Signals Intelligence, Imagery Intelligence, and Open Source Intelligence. They are categorized as either standing or ad hoc intelligence requirements. Standing intelligence requirements are focused on significant intelligence gaps that require a sustained, long-term effort to resolve and are usually valid for years. Ad hoc intelligence requirements normally involve a particular investigation, incident, event, activity, etc., and are normally valid for days or months.

International Security/Liaison Community: Includes foreign government law enforcement, intelligence, and security agencies.

Investigation: The systematic collection and analysis of information pertaining to factors suspected of contributing to, or having caused, an incident.

Investigative Evidence: Non-electronic and electronic physical evidence that requires examination and evaluation but does not require scientific examination, analysis, comparison, and/or enhancement. Investigative evidence includes conventional, analog, and/or digital documents or text, images or photos, audios, and data. Normally, one or more non-subject matter experts may perform the required examination and evaluation. However, based upon the facts and circumstances, one or more subject matter experts may have to perform the required examination and evaluation (e.g., accountant, translator, engineer, investigator, attorney, intelligence analyst, aircraft pilot, medical doctor, scientist, carpenter, or soldier).

Investigative Scene: An area or areas where investigative information may be obtained by identifying/interviewing witnesses; performing nontechnical and technical canvasses; examining conventional analog and digital investigative evidence (e.g., documents, images, audios, or data); and using eyewitness identification techniques. Investigative scenes include:

- Casualty collection areas where ill/injured people are gathered for emergency triage, treatment, and/or transportation to a healthcare facility

- Areas where decontamination operations are conducted

- Fatality collection points where decedents are gathered for processing and safeguarding

- Evacuation assembly areas or facilities

- Shelter-in-place facilities or locations, when appropriate

- Personnel checkpoints

- Vehicle roadblocks
- Traffic control points and access control points
- Family Assistance Centers
- Mass transit facilities or conveyances
- Healthcare facilities, when appropriate.

Mass Fatality Management: The performance of a series of activities include decontamination of decedent and personal effects (if required); determination of the nature and cause of death; identification of the fatalities using scientific means; certification of the cause and manner of death; processing and returning of decedents to the legally authorized people (if possible); and interaction with and provision of legal, customary, compassionate, and culturally competent services to the families of deceased within the context of the Family Assistance Center. All activities should be sufficiently documented for admissibility in criminal and/or civil courts. Mass fatality management activities are incorporated in the surveillance and intelligence sharing networks to identify sentinel cases of bioterrorism and other public health threats.

Medical Examiner: The official, in medical examiner jurisdictions, charged with the medicolegal investigation of deaths and fatality management. This individual is responsible for certifying the identification and determining the cause and manner of death of deceased persons and decedents. This individual has statutory jurisdiction over all bodies and decedents falling within the geographic jurisdiction and within certain prescribed categories of death. Mass fatality incidents may involve victims who are within those statutorily prescribed categories. Medical examiners are appointed officials. They are licensed medical physicians and can perform autopsies.

Medicolegal Death Investigation Authority: The legal authority in a jurisdiction to conduct operations, functions, and activities regarding death investigations. A medical examiner and/or coroner holds this authority.

Missing Person: A known individual being sought whose location is unknown. Missing persons also include an unidentified injured or deceased person.

Multimedia Evidence: Physical evidence consisting of analog or digital media, including film, tape, magnetic media, and optical media, and/or the information contained therein.

Need to Know: A determination made by an authorized holder of classified information that disclosure/dissemination of the information to an appropriately cleared individual is necessary to permit that individual to perform his/her official duties. The determination is not made solely by virtue of an individual's office, position, or security clearance level.

Nongovernmental Organization: An entity with an association that is based on interests of its members, individuals, or institutions. It is not created by a government, but it may work cooperatively with government. Such organizations serve a public purpose, not a private benefit. Examples of nongovernmental organizations include faith-based charity organizations and the American Red Cross. Nongovernmental organizations, including voluntary and faith-based groups, provide relief services to sustain life, reduce physical and emotional distress, and promote the recovery of disaster victims. Often these groups provide specialized services that help individuals with disabilities. Nongovernmental organizations and voluntary organizations play a major role in assisting emergency managers before, during, and after an emergency.

Nontechnical Canvass: A traditional canvass for persons and vehicles to identify witnesses, sources of information, evidence, intelligence, leads, etc. Nontechnical canvasses may involve residential and commercial buildings, schools, recreational sites, mass transit facilities, crime scenes, and investigative scenes.

Open Source Intelligence: Intelligence that is produced from publicly available information and is collected, exploited, and disseminated in a timely manner to an appropriate audience to address a specific intelligence requirement.

Operational Security: The implementation of procedures and activities to protect sensitive or classified operations involving sources and methods of intelligence collection, investigative techniques, tactical actions, countersurveillance measures, counterintelligence methods, undercover officers, cooperating witnesses, and informants.

Operations Security: A process to identify, control, and protect information that is generally available to the public regarding sensitive or classified information and activities that a potential adversary could use to the disadvantage of a governmental agency, nongovernmental organization, or private entity/individual. Application of the operations security process promotes operational effectiveness by helping prevent the inadvertent compromise of sensitive or classified information regarding the activities, capabilities, or intentions of a governmental agency, nongovernmental organization, or private entity/individual.

The operations security process involves five steps.

1. Identify critical information: What must be protected?

2. Analyze the threat: Who is the potential adversary?

3. Analyze direct and indirect vulnerabilities: How might the adversary collect the information that must be protected?

4. Assess the risk: Balance the cost of correcting the vulnerabilities as compared to the cost of losing the information that must be protected.

5. Implement appropriate countermeasures: Eliminate or reduce vulnerabilities, and/or disrupt the adversary's collection capabilities and efforts, and/or prevent the accurate interpretation of the information that must be protected.

Planned Event: A scheduled nonemergency activity (e.g., sporting event, concert, parade).

Prevention: Actions to avoid an incident or to intervene to stop an incident from occurring. Prevention involves actions to protect lives and property. It involves applying intelligence and other information to a range of activities that may include such countermeasures as deterrence operations; heightened inspections; improved surveillance and security operations; investigations to determine the full nature and source of the threat; public health and agricultural surveillance and testing processes; immunizations, isolation, or quarantine; and, as appropriate, specific law enforcement operations aimed at deterring, preempting, interdicting, or disrupting illegal activity and apprehending potential perpetrators and bringing them to justice.

Private Sector: Organizations and individuals that are not part of any governmental structure. The private sector includes for-profit and not-for-profit organizations, formal and informal structures, commerce, and industry.

Processing and Exploitation: Converting raw information/data into formats that executives, managers, analysts, and investigators can efficiently and effectively use. Examples of processing and exploitation include:

- Imagery interpretation

- Data conversion and correlation

- Document and eavesdropping translations

- Keyword searches on seized data

- Facial recognition searches involving image capture systems, records, databases, etc.

- Data mining in seized or open source databases

- Decryption of seized or intercepted data.

Production: The documentation and creation of finished and/or raw intelligence/information. This includes records, data, intelligence requirements, Intelligence Information Reports, warnings, reports, briefings, bulletins, biographies, and assessments in a conventional, analog, and/or digital format using text, images, audio, and data.

Request for Information/Intelligence: A means of submitting one or more intelligence information needs that are transmitted to members of the U.S. Intelligence Community, Law Enforcement Community, and Homeland Security Community to be evaluated, "validated" if applicable, assessed, deconflicted if applicable, consolidated, prioritized, managed, and resolved.

Sensitive Compartmented Information (SCI): A restricted access control system. It is a level of access to classified information compartments/programs, and not a level of classification. The SCI access control system applies to all three levels of classified information (Top Secret, Secret, and Confidential). SCI access is usually based upon the sensitivity of the involved sources and/or methods.

Sensitive Compartmented Information Facility (SCIF): An accredited area, room, group of rooms, or installation where SCI may be stored, used, discussed, and/or electronically processed. SCIF procedural and physical measures prevent the free access of persons unless they have been formally indoctrinated for the particular SCI authorized for use or storage within the SCIF.

Signals Intelligence: Intelligence information derived from the interception of transmitted electronic signals.

Situation Board: Large sheets of paper or white boards that are affixed to walls of the Intelligence/Investigations Section work area and that are visible to those working an intelligence/investigations operation. These boards give individuals immediate access to crucial information regarding the incident at hand. They also provide other Intelligence/Investigations Section personnel a commanding view of information as it is processed.

Staging Area: Temporary location of available resources. A staging area can be any location in which personnel, supplies, and equipment can be temporarily housed or parked while awaiting operational assignment.

Tactical: Produced or implemented with only a limited or immediate objective.

Tearline Report: Report containing information that has been declassified or information that is at a reduced/downgraded classification level as compared to the original report from which the tearline report is generated or produced. A tearline report is produced by redacting, paraphrasing, restating, or generating in a new form the classified information contained in the original report.

Technical Canvass: A canvass for electronic devices to identify witnesses, sources of information, evidence, intelligence, leads, etc. Technical canvasses may involve electronic image capture devices (e.g., still, video, closed-circuit television), electronic audio capture devices, electronic banking transaction devices (e.g., automated teller machine), electronic financial transaction devices (e.g., credit card, debit card, social services card, stored value card), electronic travel transaction devices (e.g., subway card, E-ZPass, airline ticket, railroad ticket), electronic access/egress control devices (e.g., identification card reader, proximity card reader, biometric card reader), cell sites, pay phones, and Internet cafes.

Technical Specialist: Personnel with special skills that can be used anywhere within the Incident Command System organization. No minimum qualifications are prescribed, as technical specialists normally perform the same duties during an incident that they perform in their everyday jobs, and they are typically certified in their fields or professions.

U.S. Intelligence Community: A coalition of agencies and organizations within the Executive Branch that work separately and together to gather the intelligence necessary for the conduct of foreign relations and the protection of the national security of the United States. The U.S. Intelligence Community functions as a single corporate enterprise, supporting those who manage the Nation's strategic interests—political, economic, and military. The U.S. Intelligence Community comprises:

- Air Force Intelligence
- Army Intelligence
- Central Intelligence Agency
- Coast Guard Intelligence
- Defense Intelligence Agency
- Department of Energy
- Department of Homeland Security
- Department of State
- Department of the Treasury
- Drug Enforcement Administration
- Federal Bureau of Investigation
- Marine Corps Intelligence
- National Geospatial Geospatial-Intelligence Agency
- National Reconnaissance Office
- National Security Agency
- Navy Intelligence
- Office of the Director of National Intelligence.